Bloomsbury Methuen Drama
An imprint of Bloomsbury Publishing Plc

800 658 166

Bloomsbury Methuen Drama

An imprint of Bloomsbury Publishing Plc

Imprint previously known as Methuen Drama

50 Bedford Square	1385 Broadway
London	New York
WC1B 3DP	NY 10018
UK	USA

www.bloomsbury.com

**BLOOMSBURY, METHUEN DRAMA and the Diana logo
are trademarks of Bloomsbury Publishing Plc**

First published 2017

© Nicola Wren, 2017

Nicola Wren has asserted her right under the Copyright, Designs
and Patents Act, 1988, to be identified as author of this work.

All rights reserved. No part of this publication may be reproduced or
transmitted in any form or by any means, electronic or mechanical, including
photocopying, recording, or any information storage or retrieval system,
without prior permission in writing from the publishers.

No responsibility for loss caused to any individual or organization
acting on or refraining from action as a result of the material in
this publication can be accepted by Bloomsbury or the author.

All rights whatsoever in this play are strictly reserved and application
for performance etc. should be made before rehearsals to United Agents LLP
of 12–26 Lexington Street, London W1F 0LE. No performance may
be given unless a licence has been obtained.

No rights in incidental music or songs contained in the work are hereby
granted and performance rights for any performance/presentation
whatsoever must be obtained from the respective copyright owners.

British Library Cataloguing-in-Publication Data
A catalogue record for this book is available from the British Library.

ISBN: PB: 978-1-3500-5867-5
ePDF: 978-1-3500-5868-2
ePub: 978-1-3500-5869-9

Library of Congress Cataloging-in-Publication Data
A catalog record for this book is available from the Library of Congress

Series: Modern Plays

Cover image © Rebecca Pitt

Typeset by Mark Heslington Ltd, Scarborough, North Yorkshire
Printed and bound in Great Britain

To find out more about our authors and books visit *www.bloomsbury.com*.
Here you will find extracts, author interviews, details of forthcoming
events and the option to sign up for our *newsletters*.

A DugOut Theatre Production

Replay

By Nicola Wren

The world premiere of *Replay* took place at the Pleasance Courtyard at the Edinburgh Fringe Festival in August 2017 and was produced by DugOut Theatre.

The play was previewed at the Hen and Chickens Theatre in London in January 2017.

DUGOUT
THEATRE

THE COMPANY

CAST

W	**Nicola Wren**
Voice of Jamie	**Mark Weinman**
Voice of Police Officer	**Will Brown**
Voice of Young W	**Tanya Kraljevic**

CREATIVE

Writer	Nicola Wren
Director	George Chilcott
and Dramaturg	
Designer	Jen McGinley
Lighting Designer	Tom Kitney
Sound Designer	Max Perryment
Stage Manager	Sam Quested
Poster Designer	Rebecca Pitt
Producer	Milly Smith
PR	Chloe Nelkin Consulting

Nicola Wren (Writer and W)

Nicola trained at the Royal Central School of Speech and Drama.

Her first play, *501 Things I Do in My Bedroom*, debuted at the Edinburgh Fringe Festival in 2015 and transferred to King's Head Theatre for Festival45. She has since written short pieces for St. James' Theatre RE:act and RE:act at HighTide Festival, and is an alumnus of Soho Theatre's Writers Lab. Nicola is now beginning to write for TV and her web series *Big Girls* is in development with Two Larks Films.

Her work as an actress includes *Lovesick* (Netflix), *A Song for Jenny* (BBC), *King Arthur: Legend of the Sword* (Velocity Productions), *The Death and Life of John. F. Donovan* (Lyla Films), *Spare BnB* (Two Larks Films) *and 501 Things I Do in My Bedroom* (Edinburgh Fringe Festival/King's Head Theatre). Nicola regularly performs for BAFTA Rocliffe Forum and trained in improvisation at Hoopla Improv.

George Chilcott (Director and Dramaturg)

George founded DugOut Theatre at Leeds University in 2009 and remains the company's Artistic Director. He has an MFA in Theatre Directing at Birkbeck University and was formerly an Associate Director at HighTide Theatre and a Resident Director at the West Yorkshire Playhouse.

As Artistic Director of DugOut Theatre, George has directed plays at Hull Truck Theatre, West Yorkshire Playhouse, Pleasance Theatre (Edinburgh and London), Greenwich Theatre, Soho Theatre and Arcola Theatre. These plays include *Replay*, *Stack*, *Inheritance Blues*, *The Sunset Five* and *Swansong*.

As Associate Director at HighTide, credits include *Bottleneck* and *Neighbors*. As Resident Assistant Director at West Yorkshire Playhouse, credits include *Talking Heads, Enjoy* and *Jungle Book*.

George is also the director of sketch comedy duo *Goodbear*, and comedian *Naz Osmanoglu*.

Jen McGinley (Designer)

Jen is a designer for performance based between London and Glasgow. In 2015, she graduated from the Royal Welsh College of Music and Drama and was awarded the Linbury Prize for Stage Design. Alongside *Replay*, professional credits include *A Song for Ella Grey* (Northern Stage), *The Reluctant Fundamentalist* (National Youth Theatre), *Secret Life of Humans* (New Diorama Theatre), *World Mad* (Soho Theatre) and *Ring Ring* (Gate Theatre).

Tom Kitney (Lighting Designer)

Tom's credits include *The Magnets* (Underbelly Festival/world tour), *Flew the Coop* (New Diorama Theatre), *West End Big Busk* and *West End Calling* (Ambassadors Theatre), *Astronauts of Hartlepool* (Vault Festival 2017), *Dracula* (King's Head Theatre/New Diorama Theatre/Brighton Fringe/Edinburgh Fringe 2016), *Brimstone and Treacle*, *Her Aching Heart*, *The House of Usher*, *Sea Life* and *Antigone* (Hope Theatre), *Swansong* (Arcola Theatre/Lowry Theatre/HighTide Festival/Edinburgh Fringe 2016), *Stack*, *GoodBear*, *Love For Sale*, *The Beatbox Collective* and *A Cup of Tea with Lady C* (Edinburgh Fringe 2016), *The Local Stigmatic*, *Dogs of War* and *Brainville at Night* (Old Red Lion Theatre), *Living with the Lights on* (Young Vic Theatre/UK tour), *Trainspotting* (King's Head Theatre Edinburgh Fringe 2015) and *Fiction* (Battersea Arts Centre)

Max Perryment (Sound Designer)

Max is a composer and founding member of the band Escapists. He is an ENO Mini-Opera Competition finalist, and is the resident composer for the physical theatre company Parrot {in the} Tank and the contemporary dance company Made By Katie Green.

Theatre credits include *Start Swimming* (Young Vic), *Hair* (Hope Mill Theatre, Manchester, The Vaults, London), *Muted* (Bunker Theatre), *R and D* (Hampstead Theatre), *Last of the Boys* (Southwark Playhouse), *Four Play*, *Clickbait* (Theatre503), *Romeo and Juliet* (Orange Tree Theatre), *And Then Come the Nightjars* (Theatre503/Bristol Old Vic/tour), *Creditors* (Young Vic), *Sense of an Ending* (Theatre 503), *Three Lions* (St. James' Theatre/tour), *Black Dog Gold Fish* (Parrot in the Tank/The Vaults).

Mark Weinman (Voice of Jamie)

Mark studied Drama at the University of Manchester.

His theatre credits include *So Here We Are* and *Mr Noodles* (Royal Exchange Theatre), *Captain Amazing* (Soho Theatre/UK tour), *Prime Time*, *The Bash* and *Sergeant Musgrave's Dance* (Royal Court Theatre), *Still Killing Time* and *Eating Icecream on Gaza Beach* (Soho Theatre), *Fastburn* (Kneehigh Theatre), *The Hairy Ape* (Southwark Playhouse), *The Emperer Jones* (National Theatre) and *Barrow Hill* (Finborough Theatre).

Television credits include *Back*, *The Gamechangers*, *Humans*, *The People Next Door*, *Episodes* and *Burning*.

As a writer, Mark's debut play *Dyl* premiered at the Old Red Lion Theatre in 2017.

Will Brown (Voice of Police Officer)

Will trained at Bristol Old Vic.

Theatre credits include *The Ritual of Thwarted Desire* (Southwark Playhouse), *The Guinea Pig Club* (Jonathan Church Productions), *Scripted* (Sheffield Crucible Theatre), *Inheritance Blues* (Crucible Theatre/Hull Truck Theatre/West Yorkshire Playhouse/HighTide/ Soho Theatre), *The Merry Wives of Windsor* (Redgrave Theatre), *Blue Stockings* (Tobacco Factory), *Fade* (Bedlam Theatre), *Bouncers Remix* (Zoo Venues), *Dealer's Choice* (NSDF).

Television credits include *Midsomer Murders*, *Unforgotten*, *Call the Midwife*, *Doctor Who*, *Spotless*.

Milly Smith (Producer)

Milly is a theatre producer and manager, working in the West End and on tour within the UK and internationally.

She formerly worked for Jamie Hendry Productions. Shows include *Let It Be* (West End) and *Neville's Island* (West End) *Impossible* (West End/UK and International tours). For DugOut Theatre: *The Birthday Party*, *Fade*, *Cover Inheritance Blues*, *The Sunset Five*, *Goodbear*, *Stack* and *Swansong*.

Film credits include *All the Devils Men* (Assistant Production Coordinator) and *Justice League* (Assistant Production Coordinator).

DUGOUT THEATRE

"This group bristles with talent." (The Stage)

Founded by a group of comedians, writers, musicians and actors, DugOut's work is often funny, sometimes sad, usually hopeful and almost always musical. It warms your heart, moves your feet, treats your eyes, lightens your load, tickles your fancy and swells your heart.

Taking our joyful, popular plays around the country, we perform in a range of intimate spaces – from studio theatres to country pubs - and believe in bringing our unique brand of theatre magic to audiences everywhere.

"Full of vim and great music" (Guardian).

DugOut shows have appeared at the Sheffield Crucible, Soho Theatre, Arcola Theatre, HighTide Festival, West Yorkshire Playhouse, Hull Truck, Greenwich Theatre and the Pleasance Theatre (Edinburgh and London). Past shows include *Inheritance Blues*, *Fade*, *The Sunset Five*, *Stack* and *Swansong*.

"Oozing with simple British charm" (Daily Mail).

ACKNOWLEDGEMENTS

Nicola Wren and DugOut Theatre would like to thank Stephen Black, Phil Harvey, Alison and Anthony Martin, Chris Martin, Letitia Leigh-Pemberton, Catarina Leigh-Pemberton, James Leigh-Pemberton, Barty and Hammy Smith.

Thanks to Joe Barnes, Louisa Beadel, Will Brown, Georgina Carrigan, Geoff Colman, Jules Haworth, Jamie Knighton, Tanya Kraljevic, Chloe Nelkin, Dom O'Hanlon, Emma Smithwick, Phoebe Sparrow, Mara Leah Philippou, Rebecca Pitt, Emily Priestnall, Ryan Stafford and Mark Weinman.

Thanks also to The Bakery, Jane and Dominick Chilcott, Dulwich College, Matthew Dwyer, the Hen and Chickens Theatre and Pleasance Theatre.

Thanks to the DugOut Theatre Company.

And, finally, to Tim Booth and the members of James, for writing the song that inspired this story.

Replay

For George

Characters

W, female, a London Met police officer, twenties

Voices

Jamie, *male, twenties*
Policeman, *male, forties*
Young W, *female, eleven*

All other characters are played by **W**, *in whichever way the performer sees fit.*

Note to performer: There are moments in this play when **W** *revisits her past and inhabits her eleven-year-old self. Please do not play these moments with the affectations of a child, but simply with the energy, openness and wonderment of one.*

Scene One

The stage is bare but for a grey bench and vinyl grey flooring. As the audience enters, the sound of a tape being rewound can be heard. When the audience are seated, the lights dim and we hear the click of a button pressed, stop, followed by another click, play.

W enters, stands facing the audience, concerned. The lights snap up as she is suddenly inspired.

W   Prawns!

Prawns.

That'll be it. Ate them last night, must have been dodgy. And it was late for eating. Ten-thirty. That's late for eating. You've gotta be so careful with the little fuckers. I'll call the restaurant tomorrow, give them a talking to. Just a gentle warning. I'll drop in the fact I work for the police, makes people listen. They'll apologise. Maybe even offer me a consolation meal of more prawns, which I'll politely turn down.

Prawns. Christ. It was an alright restaurant as well, not the sort I'd normally go to. I don't go out for dinner much, but, last night, Paula asked me to join her. Wanted to give me a pep talk ahead of my interview for sergeant in a couple of days. I'd say Paula's the best sergeant in the borough by a long way, probably one of the best in the Met. Knows her stuff. She's been in the job almost eighteen years and, well, reckons I've got what it takes, so she's been mentoring me. Last night we talked through this assessment centre I did a week ago. She said so far I'm definitely hitting three out of the four key competencies. That's: one – a sharp mind; two – drive and energy; three – being yourself; four – leading others. She thinks I could work on the 'being yourself' one. Said I could afford to relax a bit, let my personality shine through.

Beat.

What does that even mean, 'be yourself'?

I am being myself. I am relaxed! This is my personality.

Beat.

Personally, I think my time would be better spent going over the appropriate information. The stuff that's actually relevant. But of course, when a bit of advice comes from someone like Paula, you just smile and nod, be grateful for her time and get through the rest of the dinner. Which was nice, apart from that comment.

And the prawns.

Beat.

They didn't seem to affect me at all until this afternoon.

This morning, I thought being paired with Derek for the third time this week was the worst it would get. The staff rotation system has gone to shit and I keep getting lumped with this big, fat, bloody over-sharer.

Sat in the car with him all morning, listening to him going on and on about his wife and daughters. Says he can't imagine how hard it must be being a woman, though I'd say he's pretty well in touch with his feminine side, soppy old git. Says he's feeling sorry for his wife Janet at the moment 'cause she's pregnant again and suffering from recurrent thrush. Said he just doesn't know how we women do it with

Derek   Everything so close together down there.

W   Remarkable the prawns didn't kick in then.

Beat.

This afternoon, just as we were due to finish, this call comes in, asking us to check in on a woman who found her husband dead this morning. Suicide. Not suspicious. Been dealt with, just need to show a bit of extra support. We'd been sorting out a confrontation in Camden Market so were close enough to take it on.

We pull up. I knock on the door and a young girl opens it, can't be much older than eleven. She looks me straight in the eyes but says nothing. That's when I feel this twinge in my stomach and it rumbles, pretty loudly. Ask her if her mum's there. She takes us into the kitchen where her mum sits. Gormless. I offer to make a cup of tea and she nods.

Derek sits down and they get talking. I go to the kettle, open the lid and notice all these little white flakes inside. Limescale. The thought of swallowing those makes my stomach turn again, harder, and I wretch.

I do not want the woman to see me wretching over her kettle, so I excuse myself and head upstairs, tell her I just need to have a look around. Open a door I think is the bathroom. It isn't. Dead man's study. Looks a mess. Picture of him on the desk dressed as Superman, his daughter dangling off his arm, looks like she's about to shit herself laughing.

Reckon I've got two seconds to find a bathroom before my stomach completely goes. I turn around to see the girl standing by the doorway, fiddling with this black ring on her finger. She looks up and gets me dead in the eyes again. I swallow the saliva that's started to flood in my mouth, manage to maintain a professional look. Then she asks:

Lily   Why would he want to leave me?

W   And at that moment, my stomach goes. And I mean, totally goes. I start sweating and think I'm going to faint so I push past her, run down the stairs, go out onto the street and vomit until there's nothing but bile.

Beat.

Prawns.

Beat.

After a while, Derek finished up and came out of the house looking concerned, put his hand on my shoulder and said,

Derek   Hard not to let those jobs get to you, isn't it?

W   I say that's not the reason I'm throwing up. He asks if I'm pregnant, I tell him I haven't had sex for ages. He says he always knows when Janet's pregnant because she pukes after sex. Knew I shouldn't have shared.

I got up, brushed my uniform down and got back in the car. Did wonder what that poor little girl must have thought.

Derek straps in, wipes a few tears from his eyes. Says the dead man must have been in a really bad way to leave his little girl like that, suggests we come back tomorrow to check in. I tell him there's nothing really we can do but, okay. He offered to drop me home and took the car back to the station.

Beat. She sits on the bench.

Haven't been sick again since I got home.

When I got back, a couple of birthday cards had come in.

One with a picture of a cat on it that I suspect is from my neighbour, Julian. Julian loves cats. Can't shut him up about them. I think he grooms them for a living or something 'cause they're always coming and going. The one that's here full time Julian says is the reincarnation of his great-aunt. Nutter. Bit weird that he knows when my birthday is. Maybe one of these magical, mystical cats told him.

Got a card from Dad and his wife, Sarah. She'll have picked it, she's got a 'thing' for glitter. Card says I should come up to Derby to visit them, they'd love to have me, the kids are 'longing' to get to know me and 'they really do say the funniest things!' Fuck off. Dad's too old to have young kids. He had me when he was forty, and my brother Jamie when he was thirty-one. But Jamie's dead and I live in London so it's all about the youngsters now.

Parcel from Mum that arrived this morning still sitting on the kitchen table. Thought it would be another box of eggs that she's home-farmed, but I was wrong. Card on the top said she'd been clearing out the garage and found an old birthday present from Jamie that I might want to keep.

Don't think that counts as a birthday present, dragging shit up from the past.

Beat.

Prawns. Christ. Should have put two and two together before. Hope Derek hasn't gone blabbing to the station about what happened. Hope the woman hasn't complained. Hope that little girl's alright.

Beat.

Well, I won't be using today as an example of my competency at the interview, but at least now I've got to the bottom of it I can finally switch off the lights, go to sleep and end this shit, fucking birthday.

Scene Two

*Lights change to a dream-like state, **W**'s attention is pulled stage left and she moves there. As the scene progresses, the sounds of what she is seeing in her dream increase in intensity.*

W   I'm back on the dead man's street. Standing outside a big, red door with the number 12 on it. Rusty.

Run my hands up and down the railings while I stand on the step and wait. Jamie's lanky body is in front of me, his T-shirt damp with sweat as he fiddles with his keys. It's one of those hot autumn days. The wheelie bins outside smell like stale pizza and old beer bottles. My feet throb from walking so much. My stomach is firm under a layer of fat, sore from laughing.

The door flies open, Jamie drops to his knees, tells me to get down, be quiet – it could be dangerous – tigers could be *anywhere*! I squeeze the railing tightly as the army crawls across the floor to the stairs and strides up them. I follow, taking two steps at a time, just like him, as we pass unopened mail on the floor and dirt on the banister. I look at Jamie's

dusty, worn-in white Converses as they climb ahead of me –
so much cooler than my bright white ones.

Jamie moves faster, taking giant leaps up the stairs – three
steps, four steps, five! My legs are little so I run to keep up,
only just miss him at every corner. My face gets hot
and red as the stairs keep going and going and going until
I'm standing in the doorway of a kitchen. Jamie nowhere
to be seen.

Beat.

There are plates unwashed. Food on the floor and the table.
The kettle is boiling over and all this limescale spilling out.
The washing machine spins, starting to shake the table and
chairs. And there's a song I know playing from the radio.

*The song 'Sit Down' by James plays in a distorted way on top of the
already building sounds.*

I call out to Jamie but no answer. Go to the fridge and look
for him in there, go to the toaster to see if he's in there. This
song keeps playing over and over, the spin on the washing
machine gets faster and stronger, the chairs start jumping up
and down, and up and down until the building shakes so
hard that it starts crumbling around me and I stand in the
middle of it all calling out to my brother, crying:

Jamie!

*The sound stops suddenly, the lights snap back to their previous
state, as if* **W** *has woken from a bad dream. She behaves as if
nothing has happened.*

Scene Three

W   Got more interview prep in this morning. Wrote down a
few examples of my strong leadership skills. Went over them
in my head while I ironed my uniform. Been up since four.
Woke up in a sweat to hear one of Julian's cats meowing
from next door. Usually this would be a pain in the arse. As

it was, I appreciated the snap back to reality. No sign of any more prawns.

Met Derek at the station and we headed back over to check in on that woman and her daughter. Told him about the prawns being the reason for all that trouble yesterday, asked him not to tell anyone. He says he did tell Janet and her friend Sally, but he'll keep it quiet from now on.

We park up outside the door and watch the little girl through the kitchen window for a moment. I suggest it's probably better if just one of us goes inside, don't want to overwhelm them and, frankly, Derek is better with the sympathy stuff.

I sat in the car keeping an eye on the street. Watched people leaving their houses and heading into work. iPhones, FitBits, laptops, all on display – no one looks where they're going. Suddenly, these two kids come speeding past on their bikes, pass a pregnant woman on the pavement and in a split second snatch the phone out of her hand and make off with it. I get out of the car and shout for them to 'STOP THERE!'

Lock the door and leg it to the end of the road. Spot them turning on to Pratt Street. I call out to them as they come off the pavement and onto the road, one lad looks over his shoulder, just dodges a bus. Horns start honking as he swerves round the corner, separated from his friend. I sprint as fast as I can, radio for back-up as he runs down Georgiana Street, he's heading for Camden Town Station. I'm ducking and diving between pedestrians, trying to keep my eyes focused on the prize. 'STOP! POLICE!' The way clears as he goes left onto Lyme Street. 'STOP THERE!' He looks over his shoulder and his wheel hits the pavement, he falls off his bike. I've nearly got him nicked!

Just as he scrambles to get back up I launch myself at him, grab him by the ankles. He spits in my face and kicks himself free. As I pull myself up to follow, sirens come screaming round the corner and a police car goes after him. I keep running till an order comes through the radio for me to cease the pursuit. I kick the railing on the side of the road. Nearly had the bastard.

Radio in my location. Lyme Street. Number twelve.

Number twelve. Lyme Street. Camden.

Beat.

Number twelve. Red door.

Number twelve. Lyme Street. Camden.

Beat.

Jamie.

Beat.

I switch off my radio. The door is still red but newly painted, the twelve all shiny. I run my fingers up and down the railings and take hold of them as a ringing pierces my head – that song from my dream. Then my legs turn to jelly and I can't breathe. I feel the blood rush from my head and my skin turn cold. My grip loosens on the railing.

Beat.

Next thing I know I'm waking up with my head on the pavement and an old Indian man is standing over me, waving a newspaper in my face.

He put me into his cab and took me over to A and E. Sat with me and waited. Said he was happy to help out a police officer. I had this splitting headache and was pretty out of it so don't remember much of the conversation. He was born and bred in Camden, grateful for the Met, something about a sister.

Derek had tried calling a few times. Gave him a ring and told him not to worry. Said I hoped he got on alright with the woman and her daughter. Hope they caught the lad I was chasing. Hope all the prep I've done for the interview tomorrow hasn't all been knocked out of me.

A and E gave me painkillers and said all was fine, no concussion. Just told me to take the rest of the day off and call if anything changed. The nice cabbie drove me home after that.

Beat.

Made a cup of tea when I got in, squeezed everything I could out of the teabag to make it strong. Put my foot on the lever to open the bin and spotted the parcel from Mum at the bottom of it. I threw it away last night when I couldn't get back to sleep. Guess I thought if I put it in there it would just go away. Should have taken it all the way outside and into the dump.

I don't go in for spiritual crap but the knock on the head must have done something because I stood there and stared at the parcel for what felt like hours. Everything was fine before it arrived. Wondered if maybe it's cursed.

Then I thought, for God's sake, I work for the Met Police. I'm on the cusp of becoming one of the youngest sergeants in my borough, I've had guns pointed at me, and now I'm standing in my flat, hovering over a dustbin, unable to bring myself to look inside a parcel of old crap that my mother sent me for my birthday.

Except that I'm not a pussy, so I did. And there it was.

An old battery-powered tape recorder with a tape inside, 'Happy Birthday Sister' written on it in my brother's spiky handwriting. That's all.

Nothing to be scared of. Job done.

Beat.

I left the tape recorder sitting on my kitchen table and cracked on with more interview prep. Looked over my 'examples of bravery'. Polished boots, washed uniform. Put the radio on and listened to the news. Hoovered. Texted Dad thanks for the card yesterday. Changed my sheets.

Chipped the dried toothpaste off my toothbrush. Hung uniform out to dry. Ate a bit of toast. Took a couple more painkillers. Heard a clattering on the windowsill and nearly shat myself.

It's one of Julian's cats, a new one, black. Creepy bastard. He's just been sitting there, looking straight at me. Still there now.

She locks eyes with the cat.

(*To cat.*) Piss off!

Beat.

A minute ago he turned his head towards the tape recorder and then back at me.

Beat.

He's just done it again!

Beat.

And again!

Beat. She eyeballs the cat.

(*To cat.*) What are you trying to tell me?

Beat.

I'm not doing this.

Not going to stand here, like a nutter, trying to interpret some mystical message from a cat.

No.

I'm just going to play the bloody tape and be done with it.

She presses play.

Jamie   Hey there, little sister.

Happy birthday to you! It's me!

W *stops the tape.*

W   Great. Done! Brilliant. Remember what this was for. I'll listen to the rest another time.

Pause. She looks at the cat.

(*To cat.*) FUCK. OFF.

Beat.

Nothing? You're staying put?

Beat.

Okay.

Aright.

Fine.

She plays the tape. **Jamie***'s voice fills the room, his warm, fun energy contagious.* **W** *sits and listens, tries to keep her feelings down, but gradually becomes sucked into the joy of it.*

Jamie   It's me! Your big bro. Sorry I can't be there on the big day but I'm sending you this early – *don't* open it until the big day otherwise big trouble, massive, gigantic trouble. You can record some stuff from the radio on it – whatevevvvvver you want. I've put something on to get you started. I selected it specifically with you in mind, birthday girl.

'Sit Down' by James plays for one verse and transitions into the sounds of a train station. **W** *steps on to the bench; as both feet land, the lights change to a warm, uplifting setting and we are transformed into her childhood.*

Scene Four

W   I stand at the edge of the platform and lean forward as far as possible to catch sight of the train. My heart pounds in my chest. The seconds before it arrives drag on, minutes feel like hours, the hours have felt like days. A big hand lands on my shoulder and I'm pulled backwards.

Dad   Be careful, or you'll not make it to London.

W   Dad towers above me. We stand behind the yellow line and I watch the train announcements, watch the seconds pass by in bright orange. Ten forty-eight and thirty seconds, thirty-one, thirty-two. I rub the top of my shoe with the sole of the other one and Dad gives me a nudge –

Dad   Oi, you've only just got those.

W   There's one brown mark on the bright white Converse Mum and Dad gave me for my tenth birthday. Finally, the platform starts to shudder. I practise my best impression of the train announcer. Jamie will love it.

As soon as the train pulls up I run to the carriage door and pull it. Dad helps me and it swings open. I leap up into the carriage and Dad follows. Coach D Seat Thirty-Two, by the window. Dad puts my rucksack in the overhead compartment and goes to talk to the ticket inspector, I sneak a quick scuff of my trainers in – just so they're both a little bit dirtier. Wonder how long until they look right.

Dad comes back and gives me two Mars bars and ten pounds. Says to give one Mars bar and the cash to Jamie in case of an emergency. Says to call or text as soon as we can so he knows I've arrived safely. Hopes Jamie won't have overslept and will be there to pick me up, hopes he's having one of his 'good' days. He will be, I tell him, stop worrying. He gives me a kiss on the forehead and leaves me to it, goes and stands by the window.

Seems ages before the train actually pulls away and my heart pounds faster and faster. I watch Dad getting smaller in the distance and wave until I can't see him anymore. I get comfy in my furry red seat and look around at the adverts on the train as it speeds up. Watch the countryside pass by and eat my Mars bar.

The ticket inspector comes over and asks if it's my first time travelling alone. I nod. Tell him, now that I'm ten I'm old

enough to go and visit my brother Jamie by myself. He's
moved out of his university halls and into a proper house, in
a place called Camden. He left home last year but he still
calls all the time. Last night he called and tried to trick me
into thinking he was a farmer who'd lost his favourite sheep
called Baa-tholomew. He always does stuff like that. He's
going to be a teacher after he's finished studying Theology.
The ticket man smiles and gives me a wink, gets my bag
down and goes back to his job. I check through everything
that I've packed. Toothbrush, teddy, gel pen, diary, pants,
socks, mood ring. My friend Alice gave me the mood ring for
my birthday so that I can always tell if I'm happy or sad. I
put it on and it glows dark green. I forgot the leaflet that
says what the different colours mean but I'm pretty sure I'm
excited!

The train zooms along and I watch out of the window the
whole way, waiting for signs that say 'London Euston'.

And there they are!

I push my face up against the window to see if I can spot
Jamie on the platform. When the train finally stops I get up
and wait for the door to open. Try to work out how long it'll
take me to run to the barriers.

Then I see him! That's his curly blond hair and baggy
trousers! The door opens and I run towards him. Jamie
spots me and puts both arms in the air and stands still like a
statue. I put my ticket in the machine and it disappears!
Jamie comes over, picks me up, puts me over his shoulder
and walks me over to a bin. Doesn't *actually* throw me in.

We get on the tube and go straight to Piccadilly Circus.
Crowds of people in all different colours, bright red buses
and flashing lights on the big screens above our heads. Jamie
squeezes my hand and tells me not to let go. He pulls me
through the crowds of excited people and into a huge
building called the Trocadero! We spend the ten pounds

Dad gave us in the arcade and get in a simulator that takes
us through space and turns us upside down!

Afterwards, Jamie's buys me a Happy Meal and we sit on the
fountain outside watching all the different people, imagining
what funny things they might be thinking.

Just before it gets dark, Jamie says we've got one last stop.
HMV. CDs everywhere. He takes me past S Club 7 and over
to the Alternative Rock section. I flick through all the very
serious-looking CDs until I spot a bright blue one, with
'James' on it. We have to buy this one – it's Jamie's name!

We go over to the listening booth and put the huge
headphones on and play the song 'Sit Down'. Jamie starts to
dance as the singer sings over and over again, 'sit down, sit
down, sit down'. We start a game where you have to sit down
every time the singer tells you to. It's really hard!

As soon as the song finishes we replay it, over and over. The
two of us jump up and down and up and down in the
middle of London, don't care if anyone is watching.

*'Sit Down' plays out as she moves back to the bench and sits, as if
listening to the tape. The song now sounds as if it is coming from the
tape player.*

Scene Five

Return to the light state as before. **W** *sits, staring at the tape player.*

Jamie   Okay that's all. Happy birthday! Stay cool. Have
fun. You are magnificent. Don't forget to feed your gerbils.

Beat.

W   I wasted hours of interview prep time. Listening to
that tape.

Jamie   Hey there, little sister!

Hey there, little sister!

Hey there, little sister!

Beat.

W   When it got to midnight and I had done no work, I got
my stepladder out and put the tape recorder up on top of
the highest cupboard in the kitchen and tried to focus on my
work again. A sharp mind, drive and energy, being yourself,
leading others, being yourself, sit down, sit down, being
yourself, sit down, sit down, sit down going round and
round in my head until I felt dizzy.

I gave up the battle at 2 a.m., got the tape recorder back
down and lay in bed listening to it over and over again.
Thinking about that day. That weekend. Started to wonder
if Paula might have a point. If maybe, I'm not really 'being
myself'. Maybe I was different before. Had more fun, when
I was younger.

But people grow up. You have to grow up. Shit happens and
you have to grow up.

Jamie   *Big* trouble, massive, gigantic trouble –

W   Dad would tell Jamie to stop being such a clown all the
time. To take life more seriously.

Jamie   Whatevevvvvver you want –

W   Maybe I take life too seriously.

Jamie   Have fun, stay cool.

W   Have fun.

Jamie   Don't forget to feed your gerbils –

W *smiles.*

W   Okay. Yeah. Maybe that's it. Maybe I do need to have
more fun. Loosen up a bit. I've done enough work. Maybe
it'll help. Maybe, if I can have some fun, I'll be myself, I'll let
my personality shine through, hit the four key competencies
and get the promotion.

Jamie   You are magnificent.

Scene Six

W   At 8 a.m., I put together a plan of action. I'm going to do it. I'm going to take the morning off, go out and have some bloody fun!

And then go to my interview.

I got out of bed, put my jeans and T-shirt on. Grabbed a jumper and packed my smart shirt and trousers in a rucksack for later. Packed up my interview prep. Put a new set of batteries in the tape recorder, plugged my headphones in and tucked it in the pocket of my coat. Ready.

I stand by my front door, take a deep breath and swing it open. I press play, and as 'Sit Down' starts, I step out into the light of the corridor. Let the door slam shut behind me.

Julian's black cat sits at the top of the stairs, ready for action. We race each other down them! Cheeky bastard tries to trip me on the last step, but I hop over him! Get out of the building unscathed and shut him behind me. Give him the finger. Winning.

Sky looks grey. I stride down Holloway Road with 'Sit Down' blasting. Florist on the corner spots me and gives a wave. Usually I do the polite smile-nod but today I –

She does an awkward smile and wave.

Never done that before.

Swerve into the tube station and sort of salute the ticket bloke. Quote of the day on the tube sign, 'If you want the rainbow, you've gotta put up with the rain!" Dolly Parton. Nice touch. Wonder who writes those.

Swipe!

I'm in. Fuck the lift, I'm taking the stairs! My feet skip down the spiral stairway, overtake two guys in front of me, sort of feel like slapping their bums – if this were a music video it would be a classic moment, as is maybe a tad pervy. I zoom on to the platform as the second chorus starts. I'm nailing this.

The next Piccadilly Line train will arrive in seven minutes.

Seven?!

I rewind the song and start again. Stand by the yellow line and peer over into the tunnel. Everyone else on the platform notices me doing it and sort of shuffles forward, at the ready.

Think that might be a funny example of my 'leadership' qualities in interview this afternoon. Imagine.

I go over the actual answers I've prepped in my head. I'm gonna smash it.

Train pulls up, doors open and I jump on!

No seats.

Not a problem.

Very attractive man makes eye contact. I smile.

She smiles awkwardly.

Music stops. Shit. Break eye contact. Fumble about in my bag. Stop, rewind, play.

Train doors open, he gets off. Shame, but I take his seat – win some lose some. I drum my hands on my knees along with the song. It's a great beat. Look down the carriage to check if there's anyone from work onboard. Not that it would be a problem, I don't need to be anywhere until 4 p.m. I'm allowed to relax! Train is rammed with commuters – suit after suit, heavily made-up women in tight knee length dresses. Wonder how long it takes them to get ready in the morning. Glad I've got a job with a uniform.

Piccadilly Circus! I squeeze my way through the crowded train and out on to the platform. It's a breath of fresh air until a mouse runs over my foot and I remember how far underground I am. My chest tightens. I turn up the volume on the tape player.

Shuffle along the platform and up the escalator. Forget I'm not in uniform and call for everyone to 'KEEP TO THE RIGHT, PLEASE!'

Walk up the rest of the way. Busker at the bottom of the next escalator. Can't really hear what he's playing but he seems to be loving it so I give him a fiver!

Run up the next escalator two steps at a time. On the last leap I try for three but my foot gets caught and I land on my front at the top. Commuters shuffle around me while I scramble to get back up. One of them asks if I'm okay.

I'm fine!

Swipe out!

Come out at the bottom of Shaftesbury Avenue. The Trocadero, perfect. Swear HMV used to be right next door. Look around at all the shops opening, selling 'I heart London' T-shirts and key rings. Taxis and buses starting to crowd the roads already, honking like mad. Wonder if it's ever quiet here. Keep my headphones firmly in place. No sign of an HMV. Guess it must have closed down.

Before Trocadero opens I get a hot Belgian waffle with chocolate and lean up against the pillar outside. Spot a homeless man folding up his cardboard box, go over and take off my headphones. I don't have any change so offer him the rest of the waffle. He says,

Tramp   Who do you think you are?

W   And walks off.

Don't really want the rest of the waffle now.

Put my headphones back on and stay focused on listening to the song and looking up at the buildings around. Don't think I look up enough.

Finally, it opens! Trocadero. Loads of shitty pound shops on the way in, don't remember those. Big lift in the middle of the building – I do remember that! Get in it and up we go.

I'm alone so put my arms straight above my head like Superman but it goes slowly this time, clunky.

Maybe it's warming up.

Get out and go over to the guy at the front desk who looks up from his Android. I ask him where the simulator that makes you go upside down is. He looks at me, blank. He says,

Trocadero Kid   There ain't no upside-down rides here.

W   I think there are, mate. I remember distinctly one ride that was like you're in space and it goes upside down. Literally, completely upside down.

Trocadero Kid   Nah. You finking of Alton Towers.

W   I'm really not.

He shrugs. Asks:

Trocadero Kid   How comes you ain't at work? You skiving?

W   I tell him, no. I've got an important interview this afternoon, just trying to relax and have a bit of fun. He gives me change for a tenner and as I walk off he calls out,

Trocadero Kid   Good luck with the interview, yeah?

W   There we go! I give him a thumbs up and get the headphones back on. Do a round of the Trocadero, try three simulators! They do not go upside down. Swear they used to.

Find this trampoline in the middle of the building that you get harnessed into so you can jump really high. I give it a go but then the queue starts building up for it and it's all kids so I feel bad and get off.

Head back outside and grab some lunch.

Put my bag on my front and hold onto it as tight as I can, pickpockets everywhere. I sit by the fountain in the middle of it all and eat a Big Mac. Watch people pass by, listen into conversations. Break-up on my left, kid screaming on my right. Must be in the background of about four hundred selfies.

A little girl and her mum feed bread to the pigeons. It's sweet, until one of them shits on her and she screams.

There's one of those human statues. He's dead still, dressed as a cowboy and sitting on a floating saddle. I watch him for a bit – see if I can catch him twitching, but he's too good. Think I could fancy myself as a sheriff.

Sergeant first though.

Got an hour before I need to be at the interview so I buy myself another waffle and wander back over to the tube. Play the tape from the beginning, one more time.

Jamie   Hey there, little sister.

W   Back on the tube. Plenty of seats. Take my headphones off and close my eyes. Go over everything I've prepared for the interview for the millionth time.

Scene Seven

*The lights switch to a dream-like state as **W**'s attention is pulled to an imaginary scene playing out in front of her.*

I'm a cowgirl. I'm wearing a hat and a pair of cowboy boots. I've got a plastic pistol in one hand and a rope in the other. Jamie is dressed as a bull and we're running around the living room. He's stuffed his brown jumper with pillows and is using his fingers as horns. The beige carpet is the dust underneath us and the arms of the sofa and chairs are horses. All the pictures that hang on the wall are the spectators of this rodeo. I'm shouting 'yeee-hawwwww, yeee-hawwwww' and Jamie is mooing. I throw my lasso in the air and swing it and swing it and swing it – Jamie catches hold of it and ties it around his neck and squeals! I try to release him but he pulls the rope tighter and tighter until he starts to choke. I tug on the rope to make him let go but it tightens again and yanks him towards me, blood rushing to his face as he falls to his knees. He gasps for air as his whole body slumps on the floor. I stand over him shouting 'Yeee-hawwwww! Yeeee-hawwwww!'

But he lies there, lifeless, making no sound.

The sound of a train rattling to a halt. Lights snap back to previous state.

The train jolts and I snap awake. Can't breathe, need to get out of the tube. Doors open, I run.

Scene Eight

Lights close in on **W**. *We hear a phone ringing.* **Policeman** *and* **Young W** *are pre-recorded voices on the phone.*

Young W   Hello?

Policeman   Hello. This is Officer Lewis calling from the Metropolitan Police. May I speak to Mrs Weston please?

Young W   Hi, Jamie.

W   Up the escalators and out into the air.

Policeman   May I speak to your mother please, Miss.

Young W (*laughing*)   Jamie, I *know* this is you.

Policeman   Miss, this is an urgent matter.

W   Run through King's Cross, up through Euston.

Young W (*laughing*)   Are you calling about Baa-tholomew?

Policeman   I'm calling about James Weston. Please, this isn't a joke.

W   Through Mornington Crescent –

Young W   James, stop it!

W   Camden Town –

Policeman   Your brother is – Your brother has – miss, please. I'm sorry. Please put your mother on.

W   Lyme Street. Number twelve.

I run my fingers up and down the railings. No smell of stale pizza or old beer bottles. I put my hand on the door that used to be cracked and faded. A little sign above the letterbox says 'No Leaflets Please'. I kneel down and lift the flap. The brown carpet's gone, in its place is wooden panelling. The walls are all white. Smart, shiny shoes neatly laid out on a rack and a stand for big umbrellas. It's clean. Really clean. Not even one bit of post on the floor.

Beat.

Not even one sign of Jamie.

Beat.

It's three forty-five. Too late to get to the interview.

I sit on the pavement with the tape recorder on my lap.

The recording plays.

Jamie   Hey there, little sister.

W   Hi, Jamie

Jamie   It's me, it's your big brother –

W   Can you hear me?

Jamie   Sorry I can't be there –

W   Why did you have to go?

Jamie   Big trouble. Massive, gigantic trouble.

W   Did I do something wrong?

Jamie   I selected it specifically with you in mind, birthday girl.

W   Why didn't you tell me anything?

Jamie   Whatevvvvver you want.

Stop. Play.

Jamie   Whatevvvvver you want.

Stop. Play.

Jamie   Whatevvvvver you want.

Beat.

W   I want things to be fun again.

I want to forgive you.

I want you to come back.

Jamie   Don't forget to feed your gerbils.

W   Jamie, I'm sorry.

I need to forget you.

Stop. She gets off the floor, steeling herself.

I take the cassette out of the machine and pull the brown tape out of it, throw the plastic casing to the floor and stamp on it as hard as I can until its crushed. Leave it all on the side of the road and walk home.

Scene Nine

Some time has passed.

W   Been going to the gym a lot. Stupidly let the name of the one near my flat slip to Derek and he signed up a few weeks ago. Said he thinks, what with Janet's pregnancy, that he's carrying a bit of sympathy weight.

Not sure I've ever known Derek when he hasn't be carrying a bit of sympathy weight. How he ever passed the bleep test is beyond me. He's been going with his daughter to a legs, bums and tums class and loves it. Bless him. When he joined I cancelled my membership and found a Virgin Active on Finchley Road. It's a bit of a walk but I don't mind it, sort of acts as a warm-up.

Last week after an early shift I went along. Cross-trainer, bit of leg work, circuits, the usual. Watched this Zumba class going on in the studio with glass walls. Probably looked a bit weird standing there, staring in. Just thought they looked ridiculous, limbs flailing about. Looked like they were having a good time though.

I showered and got my stuff ready to walk home. Crossed Finchley Road and wandered through Hampstead. Walked around the edge of the Heath down past the duck pond. None of the ducks were around. I stood at the edge of the Heath and watched the traffic lights go from green to red to amber to green to red.

Then a cab pulled up and wound down the window, and an old Indian man stuck his head out and said, 'Hello again!' I looked at him for a minute. Blank. Then I remembered.

He invites me to get into his cab, to come out of the rain. I don't remember starting to get wet. Asks me how I've been since that day. I say, I'm fine, work's been good. At least I think I still know what I'm doing after that bump on the head. He laughs. Says he thought about me the other day. Wondered if I ever found the person I was looking for?

No, I say, he got away, hopefully we'll catch him next time.

'No, no,' he says. 'I remember now! You told me you were looking for your brother.'

Beat.

'Did you find him?'

No, I tell him, he died. A while ago now. The cabbie says he's very sorry, asks what happened.

I say, he took his own life, I'd rather not talk about it.

Cabbie apologises and goes quiet. Then asks if I'd like the radio on. I say, I don't mind, his choice.

A radio plays. Beat. 'Sit Down' plays from it. She listens for a moment, her expression unreadable.

Beat.

I ask him to stop the car. He pulls in on the side of the road and I get out. He winds his window down, asks if I'm alright and if he can do anything to help.

Beat.

I say, yes, he can.

Beat.

I ask him to open all the windows and turn the music up.

To get out of the car and hold my hands.

We stand on the pavement and wait for the chorus to kick in.

The music gets louder. She steels herself, waiting for the chorus. On the first 'sit down' she throws herself to the floor and up again, begins to play the game, it's serious and unnatural at first. As the song goes on she begins to find joy in the game, becoming much more bold and freer with movement, laughing. It is as if she is back with **Jamie**, *having the time of her life, totally liberated.*

'Sit Down' finishes. **W** *stands, exhausted.*

When the song finishes, the man looks at me with his lovely brown eyes and smiles. Says, 'You look lighter'. I say, I've been angry with my brother for a really long time.

But I just miss him.

Beat.

He smiles at me and nods, like he knows exactly what I mean.

Beat.

We get back in the car. I close my eyes for a second and something hits me. I ask the cabbie if he could take me somewhere else and give him the address in Camden. He smiles. I ask if we can make a quick stop and I run into a newsagents, buy a small bunch of flowers. And a Mars bar.

When we get to the house he drops me on the pavement and asks if I want him to wait. I say, this is something I need to do alone, but thank you. He refuses to take any money, just gives me another warm smile and a wink and drives off to his next job.

I stand outside the house and run my fingers up and down the railings.

The door opens, the little girl stands in front of me. I say, 'Hello'.

She looks at me and calls out:

Lily   Mum! It's that police officer!

W   Her mother comes to the door. Asks if everything is alright. I tell her there's nothing to worry about. I'm sorry, it's unprofessional for me to show up like this, out of uniform. But I wanted to say that, I'm really sorry for your loss. And I'm sorry that I wasn't all there on the day it happened. I should have stayed longer, been more supportive. She says it's alright, Derek told her I hadn't been very well.

I give her the flowers and she invites me in. Says,

Isabel   Please, call me Isabel. And this is Lily.

W   Lily goes to sit in the living room. I make tea and sit with Isabel at the kitchen table. She tells me about the aftermath of her husband's death. How they're thinking of moving. How kind people have been. How Lily seems to be coping on the surface. Isn't really talking about it much,

barely at all. I ask if it might be okay for me to talk to Lily
before I go. Isabel says,

Isabel   Please do.

W   I go hesitantly into the living room. Lily doesn't look at
me, just sits staring forward at the TV. I ask if I can sit down
and she nods. She fiddles the ring on her finger as it turns
from black to orange. I say, I used to have one of those.

Beat.

She looks at me.

I say, I'm really sorry that I couldn't answer your question
before.

The truth is, I don't have an answer.

But

I know how hard it is to forgive someone you love more than
anything for leaving.

It might take

A long time.

But

You will do it.

You will forgive him.

But

You don't have to forget him.

Ever.

Beat.

I put the Mars bar in between us and go back into the
kitchen. Isabel looks at me hopefully. I say I think it's time
for me to head off. She shows me to the door and says she
really appreciates me coming round. I close the door behind
me and walk down the steps. The sick from weeks ago is

nowhere to be seen. I put my hands in my coat pockets and breathe in the cold air.

I hear the door open behind me and turn to see Lily running down the steps towards me. She looks at me with her wide eyes and says,

Lily   I won't forget him.

W   I smile at her. She throws herself at me, gives me the biggest hug and whispers in my ear,

Lily   He's my best friend.

W   I give her a big squeeze, then she turns and runs back up the steps into the house, taking two steps at a time.

Scene Ten

Some time has passed.

W   Paula took me out for supper last night. For a bit of a debrief. All's forgiven on the interview front. She reckons I'll still have a good chance if I leave it a year or two and try again. Said I need to make sure I'm really ready for it. I assured her, I will be.

Paula   Good

W   she said.

Paula   And showing up next time won't hurt.

W   We laughed.

Then I ordered a gigantic plate of prawns.

And they were delicious.

Lights fade.

End.

Discover. Read. Listen. Watch.

A NEW WAY TO ENGAGE WITH PLAYS

Over 2,000 titles, in text, audio and video,
from curriculum must-haves to contemporary classics

Playtexts from over 300 leading playwrights including
David Mamet, Katori Hall, Samuel Beckett, Caryl Churchill,
Jez Butterworth, debbie tucker green, Bertolt Brecht,
Christopher Shinn, Tom Stoppard, Bernard Shaw, Anton Chekhov,
Sophocles, the Arden Shakespeare and more

400 Audio plays From L.A. Theatre Works including
works by Pulitzer Prize-winning playwrights Lynn Nottage,
Arthur Miller, Tracy Letts, David Henry Hwang,
Sam Shepard, Paula Vogel and more

**Live performances, feature films,
documentaries** and more

PLUS scholarly books, student guides,
reference and theatre craft

FIND OUT MORE:

www.dramaonlinelibrary.com • @dramaonlinelib

Bloomsbury Methuen Drama Modern Plays
include work by

Bola Agbaje	Robert Holman
Edward Albee	Caroline Horton
Davey Anderson	Terry Johnson
Jean Anouilh	Sarah Kane
John Arden	Barrie Keeffe
Peter Barnes	Doug Lucie
Sebastian Barry	Anders Lustgarten
Alistair Beaton	David Mamet
Brendan Behan	Patrick Marber
Edward Bond	Martin McDonagh
William Boyd	Arthur Miller
Bertolt Brecht	D. C. Moore
Howard Brenton	Tom Murphy
Amelia Bullmore	Phyllis Nagy
Anthony Burgess	Anthony Neilson
Leo Butler	Peter Nichols
Jim Cartwright	Joe Orton
Lolita Chakrabarti	Joe Penhall
Caryl Churchill	Luigi Pirandello
Lucinda Coxon	Stephen Poliakoff
Curious Directive	Lucy Prebble
Nick Darke	Peter Quilter
Shelagh Delaney	Mark Ravenhill
Ishy Din	Philip Ridley
Claire Dowie	Willy Russell
David Edgar	Jean-Paul Sartre
David Eldridge	Sam Shepard
Dario Fo	Martin Sherman
Michael Frayn	Wole Soyinka
John Godber	Simon Stephens
Paul Godfrey	Peter Straughan
James Graham	Kate Tempest
David Greig	Theatre Workshop
John Guare	Judy Upton
Mark Haddon	Timberlake Wertenbaker
Peter Handke	Roy Williams
David Harrower	Snoo Wilson
Jonathan Harvey	Frances Ya-Chu Cowhig
Iain Heggie	Benjamin Zephaniah

Bloomsbury Methuen Drama Contemporary Dramatists
include

John Arden (two volumes)
Arden & D'Arcy
Peter Barnes (three volumes)
Sebastian Barry
Mike Bartlett
Dermot Bolger
Edward Bond (eight volumes)
Howard Brenton (two volumes)
Leo Butler
Richard Cameron
Jim Cartwright
Caryl Churchill (two volumes)
Complicite
Sarah Daniels (two volumes)
Nick Darke
David Edgar (three volumes)
David Eldridge (two volumes)
Ben Elton
Per Olov Enquist
Dario Fo (two volumes)
Michael Frayn (four volumes)
John Godber (four volumes)
Paul Godfrey
James Graham
David Greig
John Guare
Lee Hall (two volumes)
Katori Hall
Peter Handke
Jonathan Harvey (two volumes)
Iain Heggie
Israel Horovitz
Declan Hughes
Terry Johnson (three volumes)
Sarah Kane
Barrie Keeffe
Bernard-Marie Koltès (two volumes)
Franz Xaver Kroetz
Kwame Kwei-Armah
David Lan
Bryony Lavery
Deborah Levy
Doug Lucie

David Mamet (four volumes)
Patrick Marber
Martin McDonagh
Duncan McLean
David Mercer (two volumes)
Anthony Minghella (two volumes)
Tom Murphy (six volumes)
Phyllis Nagy
Anthony Neilson (two volumes)
Peter Nichol (two volumes)
Philip Osment
Gary Owen
Louise Page
Stewart Parker (two volumes)
Joe Penhall (two volumes)
Stephen Poliakoff (three volumes)
David Rabe (two volumes)
Mark Ravenhill (three volumes)
Christina Reid
Philip Ridley (two volumes)
Willy Russell
Eric-Emmanuel Schmitt
Ntozake Shange
Sam Shepard (two volumes)
Martin Sherman (two volumes)
Christopher Shinn
Joshua Sobel
Wole Soyinka (two volumes)
Simon Stephens (three volumes)
Shelagh Stephenson
David Storey (three volumes)
C. P. Taylor
Sue Townsend
Judy Upton
Michel Vinaver (two volumes)
Arnold Wesker (two volumes)
Peter Whelan
Michael Wilcox
Roy Williams (four volumes)
David Williamson
Snoo Wilson (two volumes)
David Wood (two volumes)
Victoria Wood

For a complete listing of Bloomsbury
Methuen Drama titles, visit:

www.bloomsbury.com/drama

Follow us on Twitter and keep up to date
with our news and publications

@MethuenDrama